Dawn Staley

# DAWN STALEY

## The Champion Mindset

By Terry M. Vess

Dawn Staley

**Copyright © by ( Terry M. Vess) 2024**

**All right reserved. No part of this production may be reproduced, distributed, or transmitted in any form or by any means, including photocopying, recording, or other electronic or mechanical methods, without the prior written permission of the publisher, except in the case of brief quotation embodied in critical reviews and certain other non commercial uses permitted by copyright law.**

Dawn Staley

**TABLE OF CONTENTS**

**INTRODUCTION**

**CHAPTER 1**

**Childhood and Adolescence**

**Dawn Staley's Social Circle**

**Learning About Basketball**

**CHAPTER 2**

**Star at Virginia University**

**Player of the Year in the Nation**

**Getting Virginia to the NCAA Championship**

**CHAPTER 3**

**Atlanta Olympics, 1996**

**The 2000 Olympics in Sydney**

**Gold Medallists at the Olympics**

**CHAPTER 4**

**Drafting in the WNBA**

**Joining the Richmond Fury**

Dawn Staley

**Representing Charlotte Sting**

**Participating in Houston Comets games**

**CHAPTER 5**

**University of Temple**

**Rebuilding the Course**

**Temple Achievements**

**CHAPTER 6**

**Returning to Her Native State**

**Obstacles and Restoration**

**Programme Transformation**

**CHAPTER 7**

**NCAA Champions for 2017**

**Establishing a Superpower**

**Matches against Geno Auriemma and UConn**

**CHAPTER 8**

**Beijing Olympics, 2008**

**Tokyo Olympics in 2020**

**Olympic Gold Medal Coach**

Dawn Staley

**CHAPTER 9**

**The Basketball Hall of Fame of the Naismith Memorial**

**Appreciating Her Influence**

**CHAPTER 10**

**Generosity and Contribution**

**Inspiration and Role Modelling**

**Enduring Legacy**

**CONCLUSION**

Dawn Staley

# INTRODUCTION

Dawn Staley's ascent to fame is proof of the resilient nature of the human spirit. It was forged in the furnace of misfortune, softened by steadfast resolve, and refined by an insatiable drive for perfection. Her journey from modest beginnings to the height of basketball success is a compelling story that goes beyond the confines of athletics and imparts a valuable lesson in resilience, tenacity, and the unwavering pursuit of one's aspirations.

Dawn was born in the centre of Philadelphia, and her early years were forever impacted by her father's absence and her mother's steadfast love. Growing up in a home with just one parent, she was taught the importance of being independent and carving out her path. Dawn originally fell in love with basketball on the sun-drenched courts in her

Dawn Staley

neighbourhood and passion that would go on to become an incredible career.

Dawn immediately rose to the top of the sport as a result of her natural talent and unwavering work ethic when she began her college career at the University of Virginia. Audiences were enthralled by her stunning performances on the hardwood as she skillfully combined athleticism, talent, and an unwavering spirit of competition. Dawn improved her game with every season that went by, and her eventual achievement of winning National Player of the Year is evidence of her unwavering commitment to the pursuit of greatness.

However, Dawn cemented her place in basketball history on the biggest platform of them all and the Olympic Games. Clad in the recognizable Team USA red, white, and blue, she became a key player

Dawn Staley

whose clutch efforts helped the squad win back-to-back gold medals in 1996 and 2000. These victories were more than just physical achievements; they were also significant representations of tenacity, teamwork, and the unquenchable spirit of a champion.

With a smooth transition from player to coach, Dawn started a new chapter in her career that would further cement her reputation as a game-changing personality. During her time at Temple University, she instilled her unrelenting commitment to quality and indomitable spirit into the program, making it a masterclass in reconstruction and revitalization. Her coaching abilities began to sprout here, eventually developing into a philosophy that would eventually pay off at the University of South Carolina.

Dawn set out on a mission to take the Gamecocks to previously unheard-of heights right in the centre of her home state. She painstakingly created a culture of

## Dawn Staley

self-control, resiliency, and an unwavering quest for excellence that has grown with every season that goes by. Her strategic savvy and unshakable faith in her players paid off handsomely as they won the 2017 NCAA National Championship. This ultimate accomplishment was more than just a victory on the court; it was a thundering confirmation of the strength of tenacity and the unquenchable spirit of a champion.

Dawn's influence goes much beyond the basketball court. She has inspired countless people with her persistent dedication to developing leadership skills, inspiring young women, and promoting the principles of perseverance and hard work. She has had a profound impact on many people's lives via her charitable work and mentoring position, irreversibly changing the fabric of society.

# CHAPTER 1

## (Birth and Growing up )

## Childhood and Adolescence

She broke social norms and defied the odds after being born on May 19, 1970, in the North Philadelphia neighbourhood of the city. She became a bright example of resiliency and steadfast drive.

Dawn's mother, Estelle, was a magnificent woman who represented the qualities of courage and altruism. She provided Dawn with unfailing love and support during her formative years. As a single mother raising Dawn, Estelle taught her the priceless values of independence, tenacity, and the unwavering conviction that no goal is too big to achieve.

Dawn Staley

Despite the uncertainties caused by her father Domingo Battee's disappearance, Dawn found inspiration and comfort in the welcoming arms of her community. Her playground was the streets of North Philadelphia, a blank canvas on which she could unleash her unbridled energy and voracious need for adventure.

Dawn Staley

## Dawn Staley's Social Circle

Dawn Staley's relationships have been a chapter weaved with strands of everlasting support, inspiration, and unbreakable friendships made in the furnace of adversity throughout her incredible journey. From her early years to her rise to fame as a basketball player, Dawn's relationships have been essential in moulding her personality, fostering her resiliency, and advancing her career.

Dawn's relationship with her mother, Estelle Staley, is fundamental to all of her relationships. As a single mother, Estelle's steadfast love and support were Dawn's guiding light, teaching her the virtues of tenacity, confidence in herself, and an unflinching dedication to following her aspirations. Their closeness went beyond the typical mother-daughter dynamic and developed into a deep collaboration based on trust, respect, and an

Dawn Staley

unbreakable bond that was formed in the crucible of life's obstacles.

Dawn's interactions have demonstrated the transformational power of mentorship and the enduring impact of people who have led her along her path, even beyond the familial ties. Dawn has had a wealth of mentors, coaches, and role models throughout her life, from her early years spent in the sun-drenched playgrounds of North Philadelphia to her quick ascent to the top of the collegiate and professional ranks. These individuals have given Dawn priceless advice, developed her abilities, and encouraged her to strive beyond her boundaries.

These connections have been a source of great strength, giving Dawn the encouragement and direction she required to get through the challenging parts of her journey. They have inspired her to reach her best potential and face challenges head-on with an unwavering determination. Dawn has gained the

## Dawn Staley

priceless skills of resilience, tenacity, and steadfast self-belief via their guidance, and these qualities have grown to be the cornerstones of her success.

Dawn has relationships that go well beyond that of a family member or mentor. She has developed enduring relationships with her teammates, coworkers, and peers throughout her storied career and people who have supported her on her journey to greatness. These relationships have grown beyond the confines of the basketball floor and have become deep friendships based on trust, respect, and a common drive for excellence.

Dawn has found comfort, motivation, and the steadfast support that has kept her afloat over the ups and downs of her path in these relationships. Her colleagues have been her sisters-in-arms; they have supported her through hardships, rejoiced with her, and stood shoulder-to-shoulder in the heat of combat. Their friendship has endured beyond the confines of athletics

Dawn Staley

and been ingrained in Dawn's life, having been formed in the furnace of common experiences.

Dawn Staley's relationships serve as a tribute to the enduring power of human connections and the enormous impact they may have on one's life, as she considers her incredible journey. Dawn has been able to overcome the obstacles that have paved her path to success thanks to the unwavering support of her loved ones, the direction of her mentors, and the unbreakable bonds she has with her peers. She has emerged as a shining example of resilience, strength, and an unwavering commitment to empowering others.

She has weaved a tapestry of unshakable love, inspiration, and the unbreakable links that are made in the furnace of struggle over her relationships. They have been Dawn's source of strength, enabling her to overcome adversity and reach heights few have ever dared to imagine. These partnerships will serve as a

Dawn Staley

witness to the transformational power of human connections and their enduring impact on one's journey toward greatness, especially as she continues to empower and inspire future generations.

Dawn Staley

# Learning About Basketball

Dawn's love for basketball was initially discovered in the bustle of city life. The sounds of dribbling balls and friendly rivalry echoed from the neighbourhood courts, beckoning her like a siren's call. Her passion burned greater every day as the ball bounced off her, igniting a fire that burned longer.

She showed remarkable athleticism and a natural grasp of the game at a young age. She had unmatched competitiveness, razor-sharp intuition, and smooth movements on the court. She welcomed the difficulties the game offered and delighted in the chance to prove herself against opponents who dared to get in her way.

Her voyage did not, however, come without challenges. Her dreams were in danger of being dashed by the hard

## Dawn Staley

reality of living in a poor neighbourhood, yet her unwavering spirit persisted. She took comfort in the friendship of her peers, creating relationships that went beyond the walls of the court and strengthened her will to overcome her situation.

Dawn's reputation as a prodigious genius started to catch on fire as her abilities grew. Mesmerised by her easy grace and unrelenting passion for the game, coaches and scouts took note. The roots of her future greatness were sowed during these formative years, nourished by her mother's steadfast support and her unflinching conviction in her abilities.

But Dawn's journey was determined by more than just her athletic ability and it was also influenced by the important lessons she took away from her community. She learned grit, perseverance, and the steadfast belief that no challenge was too big to overcome from the streets of North Philadelphia.

## Dawn Staley

She gained a deep knowledge of the value of education and how it could change her life as she overcame the difficulties of her early years. She recognized that achieving academic success was essential to realising her full potential, so she approached her academics with the same fervour she brought to the court.

College scouts noticed her extraordinary talent and unwavering work ethic, and soon she was faced with a life-changing choice: where to follow her aspirations and carry on with her incredible adventure.

Dawn's steadfast resolve and her desire for excellence came to the fore at this crucial moment. She was aware that the road ahead would be difficult, but her unwavering determination would not be broken. Dawn started the next leg of her incredible trip with the encouragement of her mother and the self-assurance that her community had given her, determined to overcome every challenge that stood in her way.

# CHAPTER 2

## (The Years in College)

## Star at Virginia University

Dawn Staley felt a deep sense of thrill and anticipation pump through her veins as she entered the University of Virginia's historic grounds. This esteemed university offered her the chance to succeed academically as well as to demonstrate her extraordinary basketball skills in front of a national audience.

Dawn made a huge impression as soon as she put on the recognizable Cavaliers jersey. Her unwavering work ethic, together with her natural talent and athletic ability, helped her rise to the top of the college basketball scene. Every match turned into a blank canvas that she used to create breathtaking feats of athletic skill, leaving

## Dawn Staley

opponents searching for explanations and fans in wonder.

Dawn has an unmatched capacity to raise her game to new heights. She improved her shooting technique, sharpened her court vision, and developed a defensive intensity that left opponents dumbfounded with every season that went by. Her presence on the court was electrifying; she was a force of nature that inspired reverence and awe in everyone who saw her antics.

But what made her stand out was her constant commitment and relentless pursuit of perfection. With a laser-like focus, Dawn tackled every practice, film session, and fitness drill, determined to leave no detail overlooked in her pursuit of greatness. Her success was predicated on an unquenchable quest for information and an openness to learning from her teammates and mentors.

## Dawn Staley

Her reputation expanded along with her awards and honours. Her on-court exploits were nothing short of amazing, as she was selected for multiple All-American teams and won conference Player of the Year among other honours. But for Dawn, these honours were merely the first steps on a much longer road.

Dawn Staley

# Player of the Year in the Nation

Dawn Staley achieved the highest level of success in college basketball during her last year, winning the National Player of the Year award and making history. This esteemed award served as a monument to her unwavering dedication, her unbreakable spirit, and her capacity to raise the bar on her performance to previously unheard-of levels.

Dawn's performances grew legendary as the season went on. Her ability to score points, together with her superior court vision and defensive ferocity, left opponents stunned and left fans in awe all the time. She has woven together a chapter of skill, athleticism, and an unshakable competitive spirit that was unrivalled on the collegiate scene, making every game a masterclass in basketball creativity.

Dawn Staley

Dawn's ability to manage the game's tempo and dictate the action's ebb and flow with a skill that belied her age astounded both opposing coaches and players. Her presence on the court served as a continual reminder of the importance of perseverance, hard effort, and self-belief.

Dawn's performances grew more and more dominant as the season came to a close, lifting the University of Virginia to unprecedented levels of achievement. A defining characteristic of her leadership style was her capacity to uplift and motivate her teammates, inspiring them to realise their greatest potential and creating a connection that went beyond the court.

Dawn Staley was crowned the National Player of the Year after all the awards were handed out, a title befitting her tremendous talent and steadfast dedication

Dawn Staley

to perfection. This honour was more than just a personal accomplishment; it was evidence of the strength of tenacity and the unbreakable spirit that had propelled her from the streets of North Philadelphia to the highest level of collegiate hoops.

Dawn Staley

# Getting Virginia to the NCAA Championship

When Dawn Staley's time in college came to a close, she set out on a mission to make her name known among the great players who had ever graced the NCAA Tournament floor. She created a work of art out of skill, tenacity, and unflinching resolve using the University of Virginia as her canvas. She guided her team on an incredible trip to the NCAA Finals, the ultimate prize.

Dawn's influence becomes more apparent with every game. It was amazing to watch how she could encourage her comrades, give them confidence, and lead them through the difficult competition. Her unshakable faith in her team's ability to succeed was as strong as her leadership on the court, creating a connection that went beyond the confines of the actual game.

Dawn Staley

Her performances became more and more legendary as the Cavaliers made their way through the tournament's perilous waters. Her ability to score points, together with her superior court vision and defensive perseverance, left opponents perplexed and fans in a constant state of bliss. She transformed every game into a canvas on which she created a work of athletic genius, leaving a lasting impression on everyone who saw her feats.

It was very amazing how Dawn was able to overcome hardship and step up to the plate. Her competitive fire was burning brighter than ever as the pressure increased and the stakes were at their highest. She stayed firm and determined throughout. Her steadfast faith in her team's capacity to overcome any challenge served as a ray of hope, motivating her teammates to pursue even greater feats.

Dawn Staley

Dawn's extraordinary talent and unwavering spirit caught the attention of the country as the Cavaliers advanced to the NCAA Finals. Her name became a byword for excellence and a representation of the strength of tenacity and the unrelenting pursuit of one's goals. She became more and more prominent after every win, illuminating both the University of Virginia and the sport of basketball.

Even though they were unable to win the championship, Dawn Staley's guidance and contribution to the University of Virginia's run to the NCAA Finals will always be remembered in the annals of collegiate basketball history. Her performances served as an inspiration to future generations of athletes and were a monument to the strength of perseverance, hard effort, and self-belief.

Dawn Staley

Dawn left behind a legacy that would last for years after she said goodbye to her time in college. Her name would live on in the University of Virginia annals forever, serving as a continual reminder of the heights that may be attained when brilliance, willpower, and an unquenchable spirit come together.

# CHAPTER 3

## (Olympic Success)

## Atlanta Olympics, 1996

Dawn Staley was thrown onto the biggest stage of them all, a stage where legends are created and dreams come true, as the 1996 Summer Olympics in Atlanta got underway. Clad in the recognizable Team USA red, white, and blue, she entered the stadium with a steely resolve, her pride filling her heart and her mind fixed on one goal: to leave her mark on Olympic history.

Dawn carried the mantle of representing her country with unshakable grace and determination. She knew that her achievement would inspire other young athletes worldwide in addition to leaving a lasting legacy of its own. She embraced the Olympic spirit with every step

## Dawn Staley

she made, every ball dribble, and every shot that left her fingertips: an unwavering quest for excellence driven by an unquenchable passion for glory.

She had an immediate and profound effect on the court from the first tip-off. Opponents were taken aback by her agility, court vision, and defensive skills as she skillfully directed the team's offensive flow like a conductor. Her leadership was demonstrated by her capacity to uplift and motivate her peers, creating a connection that cut beyond national lines.

Dawn's performances grew increasingly legendary as the rivalry heated up. Her explosive scoring bursts and remarkable ability to set up opportunities for her teammates left opponents scratching their heads and fans in amazement. She cemented her place as one of the all-time greats of the sport by leaving her mark on Olympic legend with every victory.

## Dawn Staley

However, Dawn Staley came to life during the most trying times. Her competitive fire was burning brighter than ever as the pressure increased and the stakes were at their highest. She stayed firm and determined throughout. Her steadfast faith in her team's capacity to overcome any challenge served as a ray of hope, motivating her teammates to pursue even greater feats.

Her performances grew more and more dominant as the competition neared its finals, leading Team USA to the ultimate reward: Olympic gold. Her capacity to rise to the occasion, accept the burden of expectation, and flourish under the harshest of circumstances was astounding, leaving a lasting impression on the hearts and minds of those who saw her antics.

After the final siren went off and the fighting had subsided, Dawn Staley triumphed as an Olympic gold medallist, her name indelibly recorded in the annals of

Dawn Staley

basketball history. Her amazing talents were able to inspire a nation, and the golden medal that decorated her chest served as a concrete representation of her persistent commitment and unrelenting quest for perfection.

Dawn Staley

# The 2000 Olympics in Sydney

Dawn Staley found herself on the biggest stage of them all again—the 2000 Summer Olympics in Sydney, Australia—four years after her victory in Atlanta. But this time, her voyage was more than just a pursuit of fame for herself.

The pressure of expectation was evident as she took the court, a weight that would have broken the hearts of less gifted players. But rather than being a burden, Dawn saw this obstacle as a catalyst that would fuel her competitive fire and unyielding resolve to establish herself as one of the all-time greats.

Dawn had an indisputable influence on the court from the first tip-off. She had obtained previously unheard-of levels of skill in the game, directing the team's offensive play with virtuoso accuracy. With her unmatched court

## Dawn Staley

vision and decision-making, opponents had to work hard to stay up with her every play.

She gave progressively transcendent performances as the competition grew more intense. Fans were in a constant state of ecstasy due to her scoring bursts and her ability to create opportunities for her teammates. She has woven a chapter of talent, athleticism, and persistent competitive spirit with every game that was unrivalled on the global scene.

However, Dawn Staley came to life during the most trying times. Her competitive fire was burning brighter than ever as the pressure increased and the stakes were at their highest. She stayed firm and determined throughout. Her steadfast faith in her team's capacity to overcome any challenge served as a ray of hope, motivating her teammates to pursue even greater feats.

Dawn Staley

Her performances grew more and more dominant as the competition came to a close, leading Team USA to the ultimate goal of winning an Olympic gold medal for the second time in a row. Her capacity to rise to the occasion, accept the burden of expectation, and flourish under the harshest of circumstances was astounding, leaving a lasting impression on the hearts and minds of those who saw her antics.

The medals that glistened on her chest were concrete representations of her unshakable devotion, her unrelenting quest for excellence, and her capacity to uplift an entire country with her extraordinary gifts.

Dawn Staley

# Gold Medallists at the Olympics

She was a true basketball star, having cemented her place in the pantheon of greats with two Olympic gold medals gracing her breast.

But for Dawn, these honours were more than just her accomplishments; they were also powerful representations of the strength of tenacity, the relentless pursuit of greatness, and the unquenchable spirit that had propelled her from the streets of North Philadelphia to the forefront of international competition.

Fans throughout the world will never forget her performances on the biggest platform of them all, which were a lesson in athletic perfection. It was amazing to watch how she could uplift her teammates, give them confidence, and mentor them through the hard

### Dawn Staley

competition, creating relationships that went beyond nationality.

Her contributions to the game of basketball went far beyond her achievements. Numerous young athletes worldwide found inspiration in her unshakable determination, unrelenting work ethic, and unflinching belief in her ability. She was the epitome of the Olympic spirit—a never-ending quest for greatness that drives one to pursue excellence.

Dawn's legacy was sealed in stone as she stood on the podium, soaking in the grandeur of her accomplishments. Her name would go down in Olympic annals for all time, serving as a continual reminder of the heights that can be reached when skill, willpower, and an unbreakable spirit come together.

However, Dawn believed that her real success came from the difference she had made in the lives of people around her, not from the recognition or admiration of her

Dawn Staley

followers. Her unshakable dedication to developing young women's leadership skills, encouraging hard work, and imparting the principles of perseverance and hard labour made her a true role model and an inspiration to future generations.

Dawn Staley saw her Olympic success as a launching pad for even bigger things, rather than just the pinnacle of her accomplishments. Even though her journey was far from over, she was carrying the weight of her legacy with her every stride, serving as an inspiration to others about the strength of self-belief, resiliency, and persistence.

# CHAPTER 4

## (A Career in Professional Playing)

## Drafting in the WNBA

With her NCAA and Olympic victories sending shockwaves through the basketball world, Dawn Staley was about to start on a new journey that would place her among the pioneers of the fledgling Women's National Basketball Association (WNBA). The basketball world watched anxiously for the critical moment when this prodigy, with her unmatched talent and unbreakable spirit, would grace the professional ranks.

A culmination of goals and dreams nurtured on sun-drenched playgrounds and hardwood courts across the country, the 1999 WNBA Draft was a historic event. Dawn's name was called under a bright spotlight, and she

### Dawn Staley

entered the arena as the eighth overall pick, taking on the role of a trailblazer during the league's early years.

For Dawn, this was not just the pinnacle of her accomplishments; rather, it was the opening to a whole new world of possibilities and challenges. She was aware that her path to the professional ranks would be paved with challenges, but her unshakeable will and voracious appetite for excellence would not be quenched.

She felt the pressure of expectation pressing down on her as she put on her new jersey. She was speaking for a generation of women who had sacrificed much to create a stage on which their abilities might be honoured on the biggest possible platform, in addition to herself. She carried the hopes and ambitions of numerous young athletes who wanted to be like her with every stride she took on the court.

Dawn Staley

# Joining the Richmond Fury

The Richmond Rage was the team Dawn Staley started her career with, and they provide the canvas for her early WNBA masterpieces. Her influence was evident as soon as she took the floor, as she carried over her collegiate and Olympic achievements into the professional ranks of basketball.

Dawn was a natural force on the court who inspired respect and adoration in both opponents and supporters with every game she played. Rivals were taken aback by her agility, court vision, and defensive skills, and she directed the team's attacking play with the dexterity of a conductor.

But what made her stand out was her unwavering spirit of competition and her ability to inspire her teammates. Dawn realised that individual achievements were ephemeral and that the team's overall performance was the actual test of greatness. She developed into a role model, a leader, and an inspiration to her teammates, teaching them the importance of perseverance, hard effort, and faith in oneself.

Dawn's performances grew more and more legendary as the seasons went on, leaving her mark on WNBA history. Her explosive scoring bursts and remarkable ability to set up opportunities for her teammates left opponents scratching their heads and fans in amazement.

Dawn Staley

# Representing Charlotte Sting

Dawn Staley started a new chapter in her career when she joined the Charlotte Sting following her time with the Richmond Rage. This shift signalled a chance for personal development and the ongoing pursuit of greatness in addition to a change of environment.

She arrived in Charlotte to find herself surrounded by a talented group of players, each with distinct goals and skill sets. Her leadership skills were put to the test when she took on the responsibility of leading this gifted group to the highest level of achievement.

Dawn had a significant influence on the court right away. She had obtained previously unheard-of levels of skill in the game, directing the team's offensive play with virtuoso accuracy. With her unmatched court vision and

Dawn Staley

decision-making, opponents had to work hard to stay up with her every play.

Dawn's performances became more and more transcendent as the seasons passed, creating a lasting impression on both opponents and viewers. She led the Charlotte Sting with unflinching drive and an unquenchable competitive fire through the difficult competition, demonstrating her extraordinary ability to rise to the occasion in the face of adversity.

Dawn Staley

# Participating in Houston Comets games

Dawn Staley joined the Houston Comets in the latter stages of her professional playing career, marking the beginning of one last chapter in her career. This transfer gave her a fresh challenge as well as a chance to solidify her reputation as one of the WNBA's all-time greats.

She was carrying a lot of expectations when she put on the Comets shirt. She was getting into a legendary team that had established a reputation for being among the best in the league. But rather than being a burden, Dawn saw this task as a catalyst that would fuel her competitive fire and unyielding resolve to make a lasting impression on the organisation.

## Dawn Staley

Dawn made her presence known as soon as she was on the court. She had obtained previously unheard-of levels of skill in the game, directing the team's offensive play with virtuoso accuracy. With her unmatched court vision and decision-making, opponents had to work hard to stay up with her every play.

With unyielding resolve and unquenchable competitive fire, she guided the Houston Comets through the gruelling competition, demonstrating an extraordinary capacity to rise to the occasion in the face of adversity.

Dawn Staley had cemented her place in the annals of WNBA greats as she neared the end of her playing career. From the sun-drenched playgrounds of her childhood to the biggest stages of professional basketball, her journey had been one of resiliency, tenacity, and an uncompromising pursuit of perfection. Dawn left behind a legacy as she retired from the sport she loved, one that would motivate upcoming generations of athletes and serve as an example of the

Dawn Staley

strength of perseverance, hard effort, and an unbreakable spirit.

# CHAPTER 5

## (Guidance for Career Starts)

## University of Temple

As Dawn Staley's brilliant playing career came to an end, a new chapter that would solidify her place among the game's all-time greats beckoned. She felt a profound inner calling to share her immense knowledge and experience, and it was at Temple University that she would start this life-changing adventure, assuming her first coaching role and influencing the careers of innumerable young athletes.

As Dawn entered the Temple's sacred grounds, she was met by a mosaic of possibilities and difficulties. The program had lost its shine due to unrealized potential, and it had become disorganised from its previous

## Dawn Staley

position as a shining example of excellence. However, Dawn saw this as a blank canvas on which she could express her limitless imagination and steadfast will rather than a reason to give up.

Dawn had a tangible influence right away. She commanded the respect and admiration of both her teammates and players with her confident and authoritative demeanour on the sidelines. Her unshakable dedication to greatness and her unrelenting pursuit of it set the standard for a program that was about to rise above mediocrity.

Dawn painstakingly created a plan for success with every practice, giving her players the same unwavering drive that had carried her to the top of the sport. Her approach to coaching was a well-balanced combination of strategic thinking and a steadfast faith in the efficacy of perseverance and hard work. Her bond with her players went beyond the court as she ingrained in them

Dawn Staley

the virtues of self-control, perseverance, and unwavering faith in their ability.

Her impact on the Temple program became more and more noticeable as the seasons passed. Her teams' performance was so intense and precise that it left their opponents reeling; their offensive fluidity and defensive grit were a credit to the coach's unshakable commitment and thorough preparation.

But what made Dawn stand out was her capacity to establish a deep connection with her athletes. She realised that coaching was more than just teaching technical skills; it was a sacred trust and an obligation to develop the minds and souls of the young ladies she was guiding.

Dawn Staley

# Rebuilding the Course

Over Dawn Staley's career at Temple University, the responsibility of reconstructing a program that had once been a source of pride fell heavily on her. Even the most seasoned coaches would have been intimidated by this difficult task, but Dawn saw it as a chance to fully express her leadership skills and her unrelenting dedication to greatness.

She knew right away that the path to resurrection would be difficult and that each obstacle would put her to the test of her resolve and her steadfast belief in the strength of tenacity. She tackled this enormous undertaking with the same perseverance and resolve that characterised her playing career, painstakingly analysing the program's flaws and developing a thorough recovery plan.

## Dawn Staley

Dawn's reconstruction efforts revolved around a basic mentality change. Her players carried with them the conviction that greatness was a process rather than an end goal, requiring constant discipline, hard effort, and faith in the process. Dawn gradually removed the uncertainty and complacency that had surrounded the program with each practice session, film study, and mentoring session, replacing them with a fierce drive to reach ever-higher levels of performance.

Dawn's influence was felt much beyond the basketball floor. She realised that rebuilding a program required not only developing the players' physical skills but also their minds and spirits. She shared the priceless lessons that had shaped her personality with everyone she encountered: the value of resiliency, the necessity of persistence, and the unflinching conviction that no challenge was too big to overcome.

## Dawn Staley

As the seasons changed, Dawn's hard work started to pay off. The Temple program saw an incredible metamorphosis, shaking off its reputation for being mediocre and becoming a formidable force on the national scene. Her team's performance was so intense and accurate that it left opponents dumbfounded; their offensive agility and defensive perseverance were evidence of their coach's unshakable dedication and careful planning.

However, Dawn believed that success measured in real terms went well beyond the scoreboard. Her players had been imbued with a feeling of self-worth, confidence in their skills, and an intense ambition to create a lasting impression on the rich history of Temple University. With every triumph, every arduous conflict, and every lesson learned, Dawn was fostering the next wave of leaders, enabling them to smash through barriers and resist social constraints.

Dawn Staley

# Temple Achievements

Dawn's achievements at Temple were not only determined by victories and defeats but also by the deep influence she had on her players' lives and the enduring imprint she made on the university's legendary history.

With every season that went by, the Temple program broke records and exceeded expectations, all thanks to Dawn's leadership. Her teams displayed a level of skill and energy that left rivals dumbfounded. Their attacking and defensive agility were masterworks of coaching skills.

The players for Dawn entered the court with a goal that went beyond the confines of the actual game. They were more than just athletes; they were living examples of the principles Dawn had ingrained in them. Their performances inspired future generations and resonated across the Temple community as a symphony of ability, tenacity, and unwavering belief in their abilities.

Dawn's influence went well beyond the basketball court, as she developed into a source of motivation and a force for good in the institution and the neighbourhood. She served as a mentor and role model to numerous others due to her unwavering dedication to leadership development, inspiring young women, and instilling the principles of perseverance and hard work.

The program Dawn had tirelessly established stood as a tribute to her unyielding spirit and her capacity to inspire greatness in those around her as the curtain fell on her stay at Temple. Her legacy went beyond victories and honours; it included lives changed, obstacles broken down, and a generation of young women emboldened to overcome any challenge that came their way.

Dawn Staley

The program Dawn Staley had painstakingly reconstructed stood poised forever as her time at Temple University came to a close, a monument to her unrelenting devotion to quality and her capacity to inspire greatness in those around her.

# CHAPTER 6

## (Conquering the Carolinas)

## Returning to Her Native State

For Dawn Staley, the chance to lead the women's basketball program at the University of South Carolina in her native state of South Carolina was not only a career opportunity but also a sense of homecoming that spoke to the core of her being. She could not turn down the opportunity to influence a program's course in the state that had raised her throughout her formative years; it would allow her to leave her mark on history and motivate a new wave of athletes.

Dawn was met with a garland of feelings as she entered the University of South Carolina's historic grounds:

## Dawn Staley

excitement, expectation, and a deep sense of duty. She was aware of the enormity of the work and how it would put her resolve and unflinching commitment to greatness to the test.

Dawn had a tangible influence right away. Her players, colleagues, and the community at large respected and idolised her simply because of her air of confidence and authority. Her unshakable dedication to greatness and her unrelenting pursuit of excellence set the standard for a program that was ready to climb above mediocrity and reach previously unheard-of heights.

For Dawn, though, this return was about more than just winning basketball games. It was an opportunity to reaffirm her commitment to her hometown and to honour the community that had helped to mould her personality and teach her the importance of resiliency, tenacity, and self-belief. Dawn encouraged a new generation of young women to pursue their aspirations and face hardship head-on by sharing the priceless lessons that had shaped her journey with them through every encounter and mentoring session.

Dawn Staley

# Obstacles and Restoration

Even the most seasoned coaches would have been intimidated by the array of obstacles Dawn Staley faced when she took over as head coach at the University of South Carolina. The program she had inherited was in disarray, the lustre of underachievement and unrealized potential weighing heavily on it.

But rather than being a barrier, Dawn saw these setbacks as fuel for her competitive spirit and her unyielding resolve to restore and revitalise the program she now called home. She tackled this enormous assignment with the same perseverance and determination that had characterised her playing career, painstakingly analysing the program's flaws and developing a thorough recovery plan.

## Dawn Staley

Dawn's impact was seismic from the start. She cultivated a culture of discipline, resilience, and unwavering confidence in her players' ability, instilling in them a fundamental shift in perspective. Dawn gradually removed the uncertainty and complacency that had surrounded the program with each practice session, film study, and mentoring session, replacing them with a fierce drive to reach ever-higher levels of performance.

But Dawn had to deal with difficulties that went far beyond the basketball floor. She realised that rebuilding a program required not only developing the players' physical skills . the value of resiliency, the necessity of persistence, and the unflinching conviction that no challenge was too big to overcome.

The results of Dawn's efforts started to show as the seasons passed. The University of South Carolina program saw an incredible metamorphosis, shaking off its reputation for mediocrity and becoming a formidable

Dawn Staley

force in the country. Her team's performance was so intense and accurate that it left opponents wow ; their offensive agility and defensive perseverance were evidence of their coach's unshakable dedication and careful planning.

Dawn Staley

# Programme Transformation

Nothing short of extraordinary was the transformation Dawn brought about while she was in South Carolina. With every season that went by, she broke records and defied expectations, taking a program that was buried in mediocrity and elevating it to the highest level of achievement.

Dawn's ability to foster a culture of self-control, resiliency, and unwavering faith in her players' potential was fundamental to her success. Her teams radiated confidence and intensity from the minute they took the floor, leaving their opponents in disbelief. Their attacking agility and defensive perseverance were a masterclass in coaching genius, a symphony of ability and resolve that inspired the whole institution.

## Dawn Staley

However, Dawn's influence went much beyond the basketball court. She realised that the actual measure of greatness was not just wins and losses but also the significant influence one had on the lives of others.

Her players entered the court with a goal in mind that went beyond the confines of the actual game. They were more than just athletes; they were living examples of the principles Dawn had ingrained in them. Their performances inspired future generations and resonated across the whole South Carolina community. They were a symphony of ability, tenacity, and unwavering belief in their abilities.

Dawn's influence went well beyond the basketball court, as she developed into a source of motivation and a force for good in the institution and the neighbourhood. She served as a mentor and role model to numerous others due to her unwavering dedication to leadership

## Dawn Staley

development, inspiring young women, and instilling the principles of perseverance and hard work.

The program that Dawn had laboriously changed stood as a monument to her indomitable energy and her capacity to inspire greatness in those around her as her time at the University of South Carolina came to an end. Her legacy went beyond victories and honours; it included lives changed, obstacles broken down, and a generation of young women emboldened to overcome any challenge that came their way.

In addition to changing a program, she had inspired a community, kindled hope, and resolved a fire that would burn brightly for future generations. Her name will always be etched among the eminent personalities who have graced South Carolina's sacred halls because of her unshakable dedication to greatness, her capacity for nurturing and inspiring others, and her unyielding confidence in the power of perseverance.

# CHAPTER 7

## (Glory from National Championships)

## NCAA Champions for 2017

The 2017 campaign will go down in basketball history as the year Dawn Staley's persistent pursuit of perfection paid off with the NCAA National Championship, the ultimate prize. It was an iconic event that went beyond sports bounds, demonstrating the strength of resiliency, willpower, and unwavering trust in oneself and one's team.

Dawn's University of South Carolina team started a journey that enthralled the country as the season progressed. Their on-court displays demonstrated an unparalleled level of accuracy, fervour, and steadfast adherence to the values imparted by their coach. Every match turned into a blank canvas on which they created feats of athletic genius that left rivals perplexed and supporters in a constant state of amazement.

Dawn's ability to foster a culture of self-control, resiliency, and an unbreakable relationship among her players was fundamental to her incredible run. Her squad had an unrivalled air of confidence and unity from the minute they took the court, which was evidence of the enormous influence she had on their lives off the court as well.

The team's performances reached previously unheard-of heights as they successfully navigated the challenging seas of the NCAA Tournament. Every time they triumphed, the country saw firsthand how skilled a coach Dawn could be at motivating her team to push past their comfort zones and realise their full potential.

Dawn Staley

Dawn's team faced their ultimate test in the Final Four crucible, a task that would determine who would advance and who would fall short. They maintained their composure and determination in the face of difficulty, their rivalry blazing brighter than ever. They overcame all challenges under Dawn's strategic guidance and unfailing faith in their skills, which prepared them for a historic matchup in the final game.

Dawn Staley and her University of South Carolina squad emerged victorious as NCAA National Champions. A visceral representation of the culmination of years of sacrifice, hard effort, and an unshakable devotion to excellence, the ecstasy that spread across the court was evident.

She saw this as more than simply a personal victory; it was an endorsement of her life's work and proof of the tenacity and unbreakable spirit that had propelled her from her childhood's sun-drenched playgrounds to the

Dawn Staley

highest level of NCAA basketball. She realised that this win belonged to all young women who had ever dared to dream, who had ever been told that their aspirations were too great and their dreams too lofty, as she embraced her players with tears of pleasure streaming down her face.

Dawn Staley

# Establishing a Superpower

Dawn Staley and the University of South Carolina women's basketball team started a new chapter that would solidify their reputation as a dominant force on the national scene following their historic NCAA National Championship victory. Dawn set out to create a dynasty that would last through the centuries with an unshakable dedication to greatness and a firm confidence in the values that had led them to the ultimate triumph.

Dawn's ability to foster a culture of self-control, resiliency, and an unbreakable relationship among her players was the driving force for this project. She realised that real brilliance required constant effort, an unshakable drive for perfection, and an uncompromising spirit of competition rather than being a one-time occurrence.

## Dawn Staley

Her players embraced these principles from the first second they took the court, giving off an air of assurance and cohesion that rattled opponents. Their performances were masterworks of focus, passion, and steadfast adherence to the values that their mentor had taught them. They transformed every game into a canvas on which they created works of athletic genius, leaving a lasting impression on everyone who saw their feats.

The University of South Carolina women's basketball program reached unprecedented heights as the seasons went on, breaking records and beyond expectations every year. Their on-court exploits were a symphony of talent, tenacity, and unwavering confidence in their abilities that inspired future generations and resonated across the entire campus community.

Dawn never rested on her laurels; instead, she continuously pushed herself and her players to achieve

## Dawn Staley

greater heights, even as the awards and recognition rolled in. She realised that achieving true greatness required an everlasting competitive spirit and unflinching dedication, and that true greatness was an endless path rather than a destination.

Dawn Staley

# Matches against Geno Auriemma and UConn

Few games in the annals of college basketball rivalry have captivated the interest of both fans and analysts as much as the titanic contests between the Dawn Staley's University of South Carolina and the University of Connecticut, under the famous leadership of Geno Auriemma.

These matches were more than just games; they were titanic struggles between opposing ideas, game plans, and fierce competitive spirits. Both teams were motivated by the ambition to go down in basketball history as the best team and to always strive for perfection.

Dawn Staley

Dawn Staley, a fighter forged in the furnace of misfortune whose unrelenting devotion to her players and tenacious spirit had made the University of South Carolina a formidable force, stood on one side. Her teams displayed a level of skill and energy that left rivals dumbfounded. Their attacking and defensive agility were masterworks of coaching skills.

Geno Auriemma, a titan of the game whose unmatched success and unwavering quest for excellence had cemented the University of Connecticut's standing among the top programs in college basketball, loomed on the other side. His teams had repeatedly rewritten the record books, operating like well-oiled machines that were a symphony of skill and discipline.

The collegiate basketball world came to a halt when these two titans clashed because fans were enthralled with the sight of two legendary coaches and their rival teams fighting for supremacy. The atmosphere was electrifying, infused with the tangible tension of two titans who were determined to win and were unwilling to give up even a single inch.

The unprecedented passion with which Dawn's teams attacked these contests, as well as their relentless attacking execution and intense defence, were testaments to the values she had ingrained in them. Driven by a shared belief in their skills and an unshakable dedication to the pursuit of perfection, they played with a feeling of purpose that went beyond the confines of the game.

Geno's squads, meanwhile, contributed a level of discipline and accuracy that had come to define them; they were like well-tuned machines that performed with exactitude. Their defensive toughness and offensive flow served as a continual reminder of Auriemma's unmatched coaching abilities and the program's legendary history.

Dawn Staley

Every basket, every shot, every defensive stop—the basketball world held its collective breath, watching history being written. These fights were more than just contests; they were magnificent spectacles that demonstrated the perseverance of the human spirit and the drive for excellence that went beyond athletic bounds.

The wins and losses were incidental to a greater story that honoured the steadfast commitment, tenacity, and fierce rivalry of two legendary coaches and their teams. For Dawn Staley and Geno Auriemma, these fights were about the pursuit of perfection, the never-ending search for excellence, and the lasting legacy they would leave on the game they loved so much—not about bragging rights or personal honours.

# CHAPTER 8

## (Coaching Basketball in the USA)

## Beijing Olympics, 2008

In 2008, with all eyes on Beijing, Dawn Staley was placed at the centre of a new task that would push her coaching skills to the limit and her capacity to motivate a country. After being named assistant coach of the US Women's National Basketball Team, she set out to lead the best athletes in the country to the highest level of Olympic success.

Dawn's influence was evident as soon as she stepped onto the floor, her infectious enthusiasm and unyielding spirit influencing every play the team made. With the same perseverance and resolve that characterised her remarkable playing career, she tackled this enormous undertaking, carefully examining every aspect of the game and developing a winning strategy.

Dawn had an effect that went well beyond Xs and Os. Resilience, tenacity, and an unflinching trust in one's skills were the virtues that had created her indomitable character. She realised that the actual heart of coaching was in the ability to connect with her players on a profound level and nourish their spirits.

Dawn's advice was crucial as the squad negotiated the challenging waters of the Olympic competition. Her tactical and strategic judgments were a master class in coaching genius, giving the squad the means to overcome every challenge that stood in their way.

What made her stand out, though, was her unshakable faith in her athletes and her capacity to motivate them to go beyond their preconceived boundaries. Dawn gave the team a feeling of direction that went beyond just trying to win with every motivational speech and mentoring session. She gave them the knowledge that they were more than just athletes; rather, they were representatives of their country, bearing the aspirations and hopes of millions of people.

Dawn's impact was evident as the team advanced to the gold medal game. Her players entered the court with an unrivalled sense of cohesion and resolve, their movements a symphony of dexterity and talent, driven by an unquenchable competitive fire.

The United States Women's National Basketball Team stood tall as Olympic winners when the final buzzer sounded and the battle dust had cleared, their golden medals a physical reflection of their unflinching devotion and Dawn's important counsel.

Dawn Staley

# Tokyo Olympics in 2020

Dawn Staley was at the forefront of the USA Basketball program once more, this time as the head coach of the US Women's National Basketball Team, four years after her victory in Beijing.

There was a tangible weight of expectation, a burden that would have broken the hearts of lesser people. However, Dawn saw this obstacle as a source of inspiration rather than anxiety, stoking her fierce competitive spirit and bolstering her unyielding will to establish herself as one of the greatest instructors in the history of the sport.

Dawn's entrance onto the court had an immediate and profound effect. Her very appearance radiated confidence and authority, garnering respect and admiration from both her teammates and fellow players.

Dawn Staley

Her unflinching dedication to greatness and her unrelenting pursuit of brilliance set the standard for a squad that was about to make Olympic history.

Dawn's strategy went well beyond simple tactical tweaks and strategic observations. She realised that the path to true excellence was more than just physical skill—it also involved developing an unbreakable spirit and a group mentality that went beyond the confines of the game. Dawn imparted to her athletes the qualities that had shaped her unbreakable character: tenacity, perseverance, and an unflinching trust in oneself—with every practice session, film study, and mentoring session. Her teammates developed an unshakable link with her, and she fostered a culture of discipline and unity that would serve as the cornerstone of their success.

Her advice was crucial as the squad negotiated the challenging waters of the Olympic competition. Her tactical tweaks and strategic insight were a lesson in

## Dawn Staley

coaching genius, giving her team the means to overcome any challenge that stood in their way.

Dawn's impact was evident as the team advanced to the gold medal game. Her players entered the court with an unrivalled sense of cohesion and resolve, their movements a symphony of dexterity and talent, driven by an unquenchable competitive fire.

Dawn Staley

# Olympic Gold Medal Coach

Dawn Staley's legacy as one of the best strategists and motivators in the history of the game was more evident than ever when her brilliant coaching career with the US Women's National Basketball Team came to an end. She had cemented her place in the annals of basketball greats by winning two gold medals from the Olympics, cementing her place as a genuine icon of the game.

For Dawn, these honours were more than just her accomplishments; they were also powerful representations of the strength of tenacity, the relentless pursuit of greatness.

Fans throughout the world will never forget her performances on the biggest platform of them all, which were a lesson in coaching genius. Her teams' triumphs

Dawn Staley

were based on her ability to instil a culture of discipline, cohesion, and unwavering faith in her players' potential.

Dawn's legacy was solidified as she stood on the podium, savouring the success of her endeavours. Her name would go down in Olympic annals for all time, serving as a continual reminder of the heights that can be reached when skill, willpower, and an unbreakable spirit come together.

However, Dawn believed that her real success came from the difference she had made in the lives of people around her, not from the recognition or admiration of her followers. Her unshakable dedication to developing young women's leadership skills, encouraging hard work, and imparting the principles of perseverance and hard labour made her a true role model and an inspiration to future generations.

## Dawn Staley

Dawn Staley's Olympic success served as both a capstone for her accomplishments and a launching pad for even bigger goals. She also bore the burden of her legacy with her every step, serving as an inspiration to others about the strength of perseverance, hard effort, and an unbreakable spirit.

For those who were fortunate enough to follow Dawn's path, her victories were not just physical achievements but also significant teachings about the resilience of the human spirit. The game and the lives of many people were forever changed by her capacity to lead, inspire, and foster an unshakeable belief in the potential of those around her.

Standing tall, Dawn Staley served as an inspiration and a lighthouse for future generations. Her Olympic success was more than just a personal accomplishment; it was a monument to the strength of resiliency, fortitude, and unwavering trust in oneself. Her legacy would

Dawn Staley

reverberate through the years, encouraging people to follow their aspirations and face hardship head-on with an unflinching spirit.

# CHAPTER 9

## (Election to the Hall of Fame)

## The Basketball Hall of Fame of the Naismith Memorial

Few distinctions in basketball history have the weight and distinction of being inducted into the Naismith Memorial Basketball Hall of Fame. This sacred establishment, a shrine where the immortal characters that have graced its hallowed courts are eternally immortalised, stands as a testimony to the game's lasting history. Dawn Staley's incredible journey reached its pinnacle here, amid the murmurs of legends and the echo of prior victories, as she cemented her place among the greatest basketball players of all time.

## Dawn Staley

A reverent silence that said volumes about the impact she had made on the game she loved descended upon the assembled throng as soon as her name was called. Dawn's accomplishments weighed heavily in the air as she came forward to take this highest honour; they were a tapestry made of grit, determination, and an unflinching pursuit of perfection.

Dawn's journey from sun-drenched playgrounds to the greatest stages of the Olympic Games was a symphony of triumph over hardship, with every note bearing witness to the tenacious spirit that propelled her to these extraordinary heights. Her admission into the Hall of Fame honoured the virtues of self-discipline, perseverance, and unshakeable self-belief that had shaped her character as much as her physical talent.

Her remarks reverberated beyond the confines of the game itself as she stood in front of the gathered luminaries. Along the way, she had received inspiration

## Dawn Staley

and encouragement from many people, including her mother, coaches, teammates, and the throngs of spectators who had welcomed her as a ray of hope and inspiration. She talked about these people in addition to her accomplishments.

A brilliant illustration of the capacity for transformation possessed by the human soul and the unquenchable spirit of tenacity that each one of us possesses. Not only was her admission into the Naismith Memorial Basketball Hall of Fame a recognition of her accomplishments, but it also served as evidence of the long-lasting influence she had on the game, the lives of innumerable others, and the very fabric of society.

Dawn Staley

# Appreciating Her Influence

Her victories echoed through the institution's venerable corridors, a symphony of tenacity, fortitude, and an unyielding pursuit of perfection. Dawn's path had been a tapestry of victory and tragedy, with each thread serving as a tribute to the unquenchable flame that burns within each of us and the transformational power of the human spirit.

Dawn left behind a lasting legacy that will live on in the annals of basketball history. For Dawn, receiving this honour meant more than just achieving a personal goal; it meant that the principles of resiliency, willpower, and steadfast self-belief had been validated. It was an acknowledgment of all the obstacles she had removed, the ceilings she had broken, and the generations of young ladies she had motivated to follow their aspirations and face hardship head-on.

Dawn Staley

Her presence among the game's eternal characters was a source of inspiration and hope; she was a living example of the indomitable spirit that fires within each of us and the power of perseverance. Her journey had been a master class in overcoming setbacks, pushing back against social norms, and creating a route that would serve as an inspiration to future generations.

Dawn Staley's name would live on forever in the annals of the Naismith Memorial Basketball Hall of Fame, a tribute to the lasting legacy she had forged through her unwavering commitment, her exceptional talent, and her capacity to motivate people around her to reach beyond their perceived limits.

This induction was more than just a celebration of a personal victory; it was a reminder that basketball transcends the court and has the power to change

Dawn Staley

people's lives, develop their character, and fan the enduring flame of inspiration and hope inside each of us.

Dawn Staley left a lasting legacy that would inspire future generations of athletes, leaders, and dreamers to follow their passions, face hardship head-on, and never give up on their aspirations of greatness. Her influence was irreversibly established.

# CHAPTER 10

## (Life After Basketball)

## Generosity and Contribution

Dawn never forgot where she came from or the struggles that helped to shape her resilient personality, even as her star continued to soar in the basketball world. She realised that her achievement was more than just a personal victory; it was a springboard for her to encourage and raise everyone around her, especially the young people who aspired to be like her.

Dawn committed herself to charitable projects that aimed to change people's lives and give those who had been denied opportunities. She did this with a strong feeling of duty. Her efforts were diverse, including

## Dawn Staley

programs that promoted community building, mentorship, and education.

Dawn Staley aimed to empower young women from disadvantaged homes by giving them the tools and direction they required to deal with life's challenges and achieve their goals through her foundation. She realised that real empowerment involved developing resilience, self-belief, and an unflinching resolve to face hardship head-on in addition to receiving financial support.

Her influence extended into the lives of innumerable others with each mentoring session, community service initiative, and scholarship given out. They were encouraged to embrace their aspirations and face challenges head-on with an unbreakable spirit by her unflinching belief in their potential and her desire to impart the lessons she had learned along her incredible journey.

Dawn Staley

Dawn's generosity, however, went much beyond the boundaries of her organisation. She developed into an outspoken supporter of issues that aligned with her principles and her dedication to promoting constructive transformation. Dawn's impact extended beyond athletics and had a lasting impact on society as a whole. She supported projects that advanced social justice and gender equality as well as gave her voice to campaigns that tackled issues of poverty and educational access.

Dawn Staley

# Inspiration and Role Modelling

Dawn Staley's journey left a lasting impression that went much beyond basketball, cutting beyond the borders of athletics and leaving its mark on human achievement history. She became a role model and an inspiration to many people, especially young women who dared to dream of breaking glass ceilings and defying societal restraints, because of her steadfast dedication to perfection, her indomitable spirit, and her capacity to inspire those around her.

Nevertheless, she faced every obstacle head-on, her unflinching resolve and unquenchable flame growing with each victory and disappointment. Her experience served as a master class in resiliency, tenacity, and the transformational potential of an unyielding self-belief. Dawn exemplified the virtues that had shaped her personality via her words and deeds: self-control, commitment, and an unwavering quest for excellence that went beyond the confines of the game.

## Dawn Staley

She never forgot her beginnings or the struggles that had moulded her into the person she became as she rose to the top of her industry. Through every conversation, mentoring session, and public appearance, Dawn shared the priceless lessons that had shaped her incredible path. Her comments had an impact that went beyond the realm of athletics, kindling an unquenchable fire of inspiration and hope in the hearts and minds of those who had the honour of following her journey.

However, Dawn's influence went much beyond what she said and did; she was a real-life example of the capacity for human spirit transformation. She became a source of inspiration for future generations of young women who dared to dream because of her unshakable dedication to excellence, her ability to break through glass barriers, and her refusal to conform to social norms.

Her induction into the Naismith Memorial Basketball Hall of Fame was a celebration of her long-lasting

# Dawn Staley

influence on the lives of numerous people and the fabric of society as a whole, in addition to acknowledging her athletic brilliance. At that very moment, Dawn's legacy was indelibly recorded in history, serving as a bright example of the heights that can be attained when skill, willpower, and an unquenchable spirit come together.

Dawn Staley

# Enduring Legacy

It is a source of inspiration and optimism that cuts beyond the realm of athletics and is ingrained in the fabric of human achievement. Her journey has served as a living example of resiliency, fortitude, and the transforming force of an unyielding belief in oneself. It also serves as a tribute to the heights that may be reached when talent, drive, and an unquenchable spirit come together.

Each strand is a testament to the indomitable spirit that has carried Down through the crucible of adversity and propelled her to the pinnacle of her profession.

Her record of success on the basketball court is nothing short of legendary, an impressive collection of honours and feats that have cemented her place in the pantheon of great players. However, what characterises her long legacy is her influence outside of the realm of athletics.

## Dawn Staley

Dawn has gone above and beyond the call of duty in her line of work, leaving her mark on the annals of human achievement with her steadfast dedication to uplifting others, encouraging positive change, and acting as an inspiration and role model to innumerable individuals. Numerous people have been impacted by her charitable work, mentorship programs, and steadfast support of causes that align with her ideals. These actions have kindled an enduring flame of inspiration and hope within the hearts and minds of these people.

Dawn's legacy is a real, breathing example of the transformational power of the human spirit, not just a compilation of her accomplishments. Her experience has been a master class in overcoming setbacks, pushing back against social norms, and creating a route that will motivate future generations.

Greatness, tenacity, and an unyielding pursuit of excellence will always be associated with Dawn Staley in the hearts and minds of those who had the honour of watching her incredible journey. Her induction into the

Dawn Staley

Naismith Memorial Basketball Hall of Fame was a celebration of her long-lasting influence on the lives of numerous people and the fabric of society as a whole, in addition to acknowledging her athletic brilliance.

Dawn's legacy will keep empowering and inspiring people, acting as a lighthouse of hope for those who dare to dream and a reminder of the unquenchable spark that every one of us has within. Her path is a work of human achievement, a symphony of resiliency, endurance, and unflinching self-belief that will inspire future generations.

Dawn Staley

# CONCLUSION

Dawn's influence extends beyond athletics and into the fields of mentoring, empowerment, and leadership. Her relentless dedication to bringing about positive change, nourishing the aspirations of countless others, and acting as a source of inspiration and hope has had a lasting impression on everyone she has come into contact with.

Dawn has personified the champion mindset in both her words and deeds: an unrelenting drive for excellence that is fed by an enduring inner fire. Her path has been a symphony of triumph over adversity that resonates with a ringing clarity, demonstrating the transformational power of the human spirit.

## Dawn Staley

From her quick ascent to fame as a college athlete to her groundbreaking achievements as a professional athlete, Dawn's journey has been filled with setbacks that would have broken the hearts of lesser people. She broke through social barriers and glass ceilings by facing every obstacle head-on with an unflinching belief in her ability and an unwavering drive.

Her election into the Naismith Memorial Basketball Hall of Fame is a remarkable accomplishment that honours both her unmatched talent and the long-lasting influence she has had on the sport she adores. But Dawn's real legacy is found in the innumerable lives she has impacted, the aspirations she has inspired, and the lasting impression she has made on society. It goes far beyond the recognition and admiration of her followers.

Dawn has illuminated the path for future generations via her philanthropic endeavours, mentorship programs, and persistent support of issues that align with her principles.

## Dawn Staley

Her story is a master class in overcoming hardship, pushing back against social norms, and creating a path that will inspire and empower others who dare to dream.

Dawn Staley's legacy will endure, inspiring and empowering generations to come as a reminder of the heights that can be reached when skill, perseverance, and an unquenchable spirit come together. Her victories will resonate through the ages. Her narrative has become part of the human achievement tapestry, a symphony of resiliency, tenacity, and steadfast self-belief that will continue to inspire future generations.

Dawn Staley's name will go down in basketball history alongside the greats of the sport, indisputable evidence of the lasting legacy she has created with her unwavering dedication, unmatched talent, and capacity to motivate people around her to achieve beyond their own perceived boundaries. Her actual influence, however, goes far beyond the courtroom, becoming woven into the fabric

Dawn Staley

of human experience and acting as a ray of hope for anybody who dares to follow their aspirations and face hardship head-on.

A monument to the transforming power of the champion mindset, which is an unwavering pursuit of excellence fuelled by an inexhaustible flame that burns inside each of us, Dawn Staley's path has been a masterpiece of human achievement.

Made in the USA
Monee, IL
16 May 2025

17595167R00059